Bilingual Picture Dictionaries

# My First Book of
# Spanish
# Words

by Katy R. Kudela

Translator: Translations.com

apple
**la manzana**
(man-THAH-nah)

raintree
a Capstone company — publishers for children

# Contents

How to use this dictionary ........... 3

**Family** ........................................ 4
**Body** .......................................... 6
**Clothes** ...................................... 8
**Toys** ..........................................10
**Bedroom** ................................... 12
**Bathroom** .................................. 14
**Kitchen** ..................................... 16
**Food** .......................................... 18
**Farm** ......................................... 20
**Garden** ...................................... 22
**Colours** ..................................... 24
**Classroom** .................................. 26
**City** ........................................... 28
**Numbers** ................................... 30
**Useful phrases** ......................... 30

Find out more ............................... 31
Websites ....................................... 31

# How to use this dictionary

This book is full of useful words in both Spanish and English. The English word appears first, followed by the Spanish word. Look below each Spanish word for help to sound it out. Try reading the words aloud.

Topic heading in English

English: **body**

Spanish: **el cuerpo** (CWAIR-poh)

hair
**el pelo**
(PAY-loh)

head
**la cabeza**
(kah-BAY-sah)

nose
**la nariz**
(nah-REES)

ear
**la oreja**
(o-RAY-hah)

eye
**el ojo**
(OH-hoh)

mouth
**la boca**
(BOH-kah)

leg
**la pierna**
(pee-AIR-nah)

arm
**el brazo**
(BRAH-soh)

hand
**la mano**
(MAH-noh)

foot
**el pie**
(pee-AY)

6

7

Topic heading in Spanish

Word in English
**Word in Spanish**
(pronunciation)

Notes about the Spanish language

The Spanish language usually includes "el", "la", "los" and "las" before nouns. These all mean "the" in Spanish. The pronunciations for these articles are below.

**el** (ehl)          **los** (lohs)

**la** (lah)          **las** (lahs)

**3**

uncle
**el tío**
(TEE-oh)

mother
**la mamá**
(mah-MAH)

cousin
**el primo**
(PREE-moh)

aunt
**la tía**
(TEE-ah)

baby
**el bebé**
(bay-BAY)

grandmother
**la abuela**
(ah-BWAY-lah)

father
**el papá**
(pah-PAH)

grandfather
**el abuelo**
(ah-BWAY-loh)

sister
**la hermana**
(air-MAH-nah)

brother
**el hermano**
(air-MAH-noh)

**5**

hair
**el pelo**
(PAY-loh)

head
**la cabeza**
(kah-bay-tha)

nose
**la nariz**
(nah-REETH)

ear
**la oreja**
(o-RAY-hah)

mouth
**la boca**
(BOH-kah)

eye
**el ojo**
(OH-hoh)

arm
**el brazo**
(BRAH-thoh)

hand
**la mano**
(MAH-noh)

leg
**la pierna**
(pee-AIR-nah)

foot
**el pie**
(pee-AY)

pyjamas
**el pijama**
(pee-HAH-mah)

coat
**el abrigo**
(ah-BREE-goh)

shorts
**los pantalones cortos**
(pahn-tah-LOH-ness KOR-tohs)

boot
**la bota**
(BOH-tah)

8

shoe
**el zapato**
(sah-PAH-toh)

hat
**el sombrero**
(sohm-BRAY-roh)

trousers
**los pantalones**
(pahn-tah-LOH-ness)

sock
**el calcetín**
(kal-thay-TEEN)

dress
**el vestido**
(ves-TEE-doh)

shirt
**la camisa**
(kah-MEE-sah)

**9**

kite
**la cometa**
(koh-MAY-tah)

doll
**la muñeca**
(moo-NYAY-kah)

puzzle
**el rompecabezas**
(rohm-pay-kah-BAY-thas)

train
**el tren**
(trayn)

wagon
**el carro**
(KAHR-roh)

puppet
**el títere**
(TEE-tay-ray)

skateboard
**el monopatín**
(moh-nouh-pah-TEEN)

skipping rope
**la cuerda de saltar**
(KWAIR-dah day sahl-TAHR)

ball
**la pelota**
(pay-LOH-tah)

bat
**el bate**
(BAH-tay)

window
**la ventana**
(ven-TAH-nah)

picture
**el cuadro**
(KWAH-droh)

lamp
**la lámpara**
(LAHM-pah-rah)

chest of
drawers
**la cómoda**
(KOH-moh-dah)

curtain
**la cortina**
(kor-TEE-nah)

blanket
**la sábana**
(SAH-bah-nah)

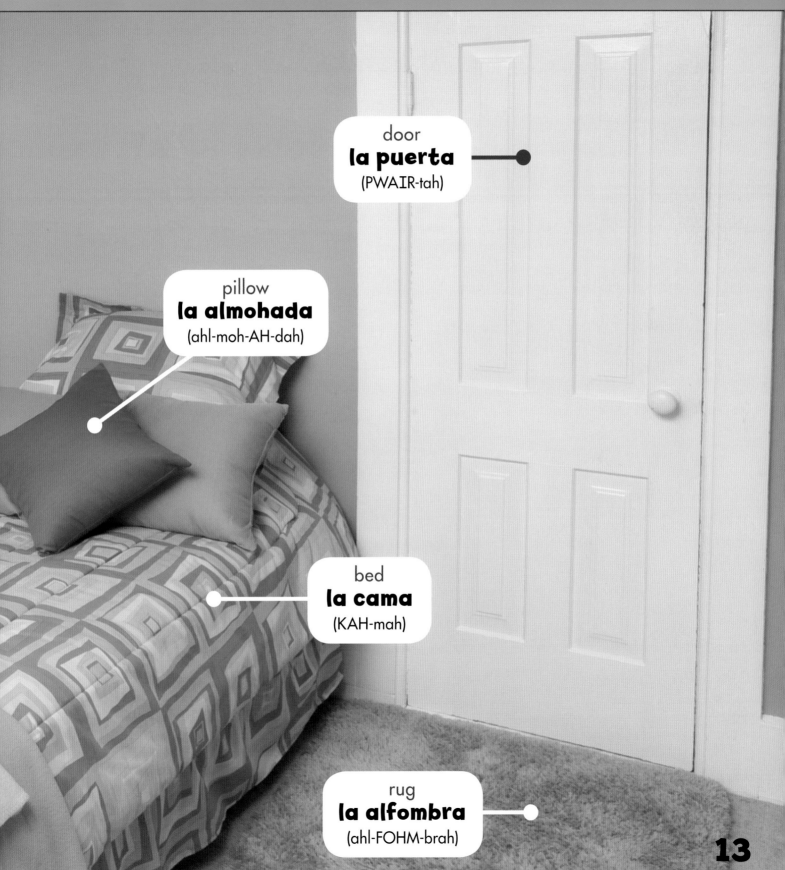

door
**la puerta**
(PWAIR-tah)

pillow
**la almohada**
(ahl-moh-AH-dah)

bed
**la cama**
(KAH-mah)

rug
**la alfombra**
(ahl-FOHM-brah)

bath
**la bañera**
(bah-NYAY-rah)

soap
**el jabón**
(hah-BONE)

toilet
**el inodoro**
(in-oh-DOH-roh)

mirror
**el espejo**
(es-PAY-hoh)

toothbrush
**el cepillo de dientes**
(thay-PEE-yoh day dee-EN-tays)

toothpaste
**la pasta de dientes**
(PAHS-tah day dee-EN-tays)

comb
**el peine**
(PAY-ee-nay)

sink
**el lavabo**
(lah-BAH-boh)

towel
**la toalla**
(toh-AH-yah)

brush
**el cepillo**
(thay-PEE-yoh)

**15**

pot
**la olla**
(OY-yah)

hob
**los fuegos**
(FUEY-ghos)

bowl
**el tazón**
(tah-THONE)

oven
**el horno**
(OR-noh)

refrigerator
**el refrigerador**
(ray-free-hay-rah-DOR)

knife
**el cuchillo**
(koo-CHEE-yoh)

table
**la mesa**
(MAY-sah)

plate
**el plato**
(PLAH-toh)

spoon
**la cuchara**
(koo-CHAH-rah)

fork
**el tenedor**
(tay-nay-DOR)

milk
**la leche**
(LAY-chay)

carrot
**la zanahoria**
(thah-nah-OH-ree-ah)

bread
**el pan**
(pahn)

apple
**la manzana**
(mahn-THAH-nah)

butter
**la mantequilla**
(mahn-tay-KEY-yah)

Salted Sweet Cream
Butter
NET WT 4 OZ (1/4 LB) 113.4 g

Salted Sweet Cream
Butter
NET WT 4 OZ (1/4 LB) 113.4 g

egg
**el huevo**
(WAY-voh)

pea
**el guisante**
(gee-SAYN-tay)

orange
**la naranja**
(nah-RAHN-hah)

sandwich
**el sándwich**
(SAHND-weech)

rice
**el arroz**
(ahr-ROHTH)

tractor
**el tractor**
(trak-TOR)

hay
**el heno**
(AY-noh)

fence
**la cerca**
(SAIR-kah)

farmer
**el granjero**
(grahn-HAY-roh)

sheep
**la oveja**
(oh-VAY-hah)

pig
**el cerdo**
(THAIR-doh)

horse
**el caballo**
(kah-BAH-yoh)

barn
**el establo**
(es-TAH-bloh)

cow
**la vaca**
(VAH-kah)

chicken
**el pollo**
(POY-yoh)

21

leaf
**la hoja**
(OH-hah)

butterfly
**la mariposa**
(mah-ree-POH-sah)

flower
**la flor**
(flor)

trowel
**la pala**
(PAH-lah)

bird
**el pájaro**
(PAH-hah-roh)

worm
**la lombriz**
(lom-BREETH)

22

plant
**la planta**
(PLAHN-tah)

grass
**el césped**
(THES-pehd)

soil
**la tierra**
(tee-AIR-rah)

seed
**la semilla**
(say-MEE-yah)

purple
**el violeta**
(vee-oh-LAY-tah)

brown
**el marrón**
(mar-RONE)

orange
**el anaranjado**
(ah-nah-rahn-HAH-noh)

white
**el blanco**
(BLAHN-koh)

red
**el rojo**
(ROH-hoh)

black
**el negro**
(NAY-groh)

24

blue
**el azul**
(ah-THOOL)

pink
**el rosado**
(roh-SAH-doh)

yellow
**el amarillo**
(ah-mah-REE-yoh)

green
**el verde**
(VAIR-day)

**25**

teacher
**la maestra**
(mah-ES-trah)

book
**el libro**
(LEE-broh)

crayon
**el crayón**
(krah-YONE)

desk
**el escritorio**
(es-kree-TOH-ree-oh)

pencil
**el lápiz**
(LAH-peeth)

clock
**el reloj**
(ray-LOH)

map
**el mapa**
(MAH-pah)

computer
**el ordenador**
(or-dei-nah-DOR)

chair
**la silla**
(SEE-yah)

paper
**el papel**
(pah-PEHL)

**27**

traffic light
**el semáforo**
(say-MAH-for-oh)

library
**la biblioteca**
(bee-blee-oh-TAY-kah)

shop
**la tienda**
(tee-EN-dah)

LIBRARY

ONE WAY

Tuesday 2:00-5:00
Thursday 2:00-6:00

bicycle
**la bicicleta**
(bee-thee-KLAY-tah)

car
**el automóvil**
(ow-toh-MOH-veel)

**28**

tree
**el árbol**
(AR-bol)

bus
**el autobús**
(ow-toh-BOOS)

park
**el parque**
(PAR-kay)

street
**la calle**
(KAH-yay)

sign
**la señal**
(seh-NYAHL)

**29**

## Numbers • Los números (NOO-may-rohs)

1. one • **el uno** (OO-noh)
2. two • **el dos** (dose)
3. three • **el tres** (trays)
4. four • **el cuatro** (KWAH-troh)
5. five • **el cinco** (THEEN-koh)

6. six • **el seis** (SAY-ees)
7. seven • **el siete** (see-AY-tay)
8. eight • **el ocho** (OH-choh)
9. nine • **el nueve** (noo-AY-vay)
10. ten • **el diez** (dee-EHTH)

## Useful phrases • Frases útiles (FRAH-ses OO-teel-es)

yes • **sí** (see)

no • **no** (noh)

hello • **hola** (OH-lah)

goodbye • **adiós** (ah-dee-OHS)

good morning • **buenos días** (BWEN-ohs DEE-ahs)

goodnight • **buenas noches** (BWEN-ahs NOH-chays)

please • **por favor** (por fah-VOR)

thank you • **gracias** (GRAH-thee-ahs)

excuse me • **permiso** (pair-MEE-soh)

My name is _____. • **Me llamo _____.** (may YAH-moh)

# Find out more

Look up more Spanish words in these books:

*Collins Very First Spanish Dictionary* (Collins, 2014)

*My First Picture Dictionary: Spanish-English*, Isabel Carril (Wayland, 2008)

*The Usborne Very First Dictionary in Spanish*, Felicity Brooks and Caroline Young (Usborne, 2009)

# Websites

Visit these websites to learn more Spanish words:

http://www.123teachme.com/learn_spanish/spanish_for_children

http://www.bbc.co.uk/schools/primarylanguages/spanish/

http://www.enchantedlearning.com/Dictionary.html

Raintree is an imprint of Capstone Global Library Limited, a company incorporated in England and Wales having its registered office at 7 Pilgrim Street, London, EC4V 6LB – Registered company number: 6695582

www.raintree.co.uk
myorders@raintree.co.uk

Designed by Lori Bye
Picture research by Wanda Winch
Production by Eric Manske
Originated by Capstone Global Library Ltd
Printed and bound in China

ISBN 978 1 474 70690 2
19 18 17 16 15
10 9 8 7 6 5 4 3 2 1

**British Library Cataloguing in Publication Data**
A full catalogue record for this book is available from the British Library.

**Acknowledgements**
We would like to thank the following for permission to reproduce photographs: Capstone Studio/Gary Sundermeyer, 20 (farmer with tractor, pig); Capstone Studio/Karon Dubke, cover (ball, sock), 1, 3, 4-5, 6-7, 8-9, 10-11, 12-13, 14-15, 16-17, 18-19, 22-23, 24-25, 26-27; Image Farm, back cover, 1, 2, 31, 32 (design elements); iStockphoto/Andrew Gentry, 28 (main street); Photodisc, cover (flower); Shutterstock/Adrian Matthiassen, cover (butterfly); David Hughes, 20 (hay); Eric Isselee, cover (horse), 20-21 (horse); hamurishi, 28 (bike); Ievgeniia Tikhonova, 21 (chickens); Jim Mills, 29 (stop sign); Kelli Westfal, 28 (traffic light); Margo Harrison, 20 (sheep); MaxPhoto, 21 (cow and calf); Melinda Fawver, 29 (bus); Robert Elias, 20-21 (barn, fence); Vladimir Mucibabic, 28-29 (city skyline).

Every effort has been made to contact copyright holders of material reproduced in this book. Any omissions will be rectified in subsequent printings if notice is given to the publisher.

All the internet addresses (URLs) given in this book were valid at the time of going to press. However, due to the dynamic nature of the internet, some addresses may have changed, or sites may have changed or ceased to exist since publication. While the author and publisher regret any inconvenience this may cause readers, no responsibility for any such changes can be accepted by either the author or the publisher.

### Note to parents, teachers and librarians

Learning to speak a second language at a young age has been shown to improve overall academic performance, boost problem-solving ability and foster an appreciation for other cultures. Early exposure to language skills provides a strong foundation for other subject areas, including maths and reasoning. Introducing children to a second language can help to lay the groundwork for future academic success and cultural awareness.